REALISTIC MAN — SHATTERED REFLECTION:

Examining a Depressed Poetic Past

by

Keith Sudak

Illustrations
by
Judy Vandeventer

Dorrance Publishing Co
585 Alpha Drive
Suite 103
Pittsburgh, PA 15238
Visit our website at *www.dorrancebookstore.com*

ISBN: 978-1-6491-3309-0
eISBN: 978-1-6491-3276-5

Acknowledgment

To my family for never letting go, to all those I've tried to pull down with me, to my wife for her supportive hold.

CONTENTS

PREFACE vii

INTRODUCTION ix

FOR ALL PEOPLE OF HEART 2

CAMPFIRE 4

THE JUNKYARD 6

THE ALMIGHTY 8

SANTA DIDN'T FORGET 10

BILLBOARDS 12

FALL OF A CHAMPION 14

DAZED AND CONFUSED 16

SADNESS IS 18

RIVER'S FRIEND 20

A PLEA FOR LOVE 22

WINTER'S NIGHT 24

ESCAPING 26

THE LETTER 28

WATERS 30

FORGIVENESS 32

SUNSET 34

JUDGMENT OF SOCIETY 36

LOOK UNDER THE BUSHES 38

PIERCING THE DARKNESS 44

Original 1977 Book Cover

1977 PREFACE

This book holds bits and pieces of anger, wishes, memories, joys, and sorrows, for our minds contain true but subdued feelings of living and share the indecision of its purpose.

In today's world of carbon-copy people and tedious communication, a person must escape the routines to experience a realistic view of existence. If we could always be individual. More often our lives are floating pools of limbo where words and faces are as common as the blades of grass.

Novelist Thomas Wolf expressed it: "Which one of us has known his brother? Which of us has looked into his father's heart? Which of us has not remained forever prison-pent? Which of us is not forever a stranger and alone?" The world is a lonely place.

Existence means many things to many people. Existence can be a career, family, faith, wealth, fame or a just few moments of peace. They all provide purpose. Sit back and let the moment surrender a conscious and honest opinion of our position.

INTRODUCTION

This book explores bits and pieces of an undiagnosed depressive period of my life and compared them to a new reality. I expressed my personal deep thoughts, with poems and short stories, while existing with depression during these writings and for much of my life. Depression and anxiety gradually eroded my soul, alienated family, crippled learning, sabotaged employment, and triggered serious health issues. It was only after the diagnosis of clinical depression and panic disorder that I was able to begin my recovery, revealing a world of lost emotions and a joyful understanding of self. Perhaps my reflections of these writings will enlighten those suffering with depression.

To quote Dutch painter Vincent van Gogh: "Though I am often in the depths of misery, there is still calmness, pure harmony and music inside me...."

Embrace these painful verses as potential doors to your happiness. The following reflections provide insight to those suffering with depression.

REALISTIC MAN — SHATTERED REFLECTION:

Examining a Depressed Poetic Past

FOR ALL PEOPLE OF HEART

My tear-glazed eyes
Cry out to the blackened skies.

How painfully lonely they are
Searching for a needing star.

Curious fingers grasp blades of grass
Seeking mind ponders its tiny mass.

Restless waves collapse upon the shore
The anxious solitude tears at my core.

Agonizing memories begin creeping up
My heart bleeds, stabbing thoughts cut.

Being a man who needs no 'cane
Ways are realistic, feeling no pain.

A convinced mind tilts to blackened skies
And a tear trickles from my realistic eyes.

FOR ALL PEOPLE OF HEART *begins the collection of works written while battling depression and anxiety. This poem describes the struggle to recognize reality while peering through the fog of mental illness. Flashes of hope become overtaken by the opposing thoughts of desperation. Survival succumbs to sadness and denies happiness.*

I became more or less housebound during the reign of depression and anxiety. Travel was sporadic and only took place on the good days. Simple activities such as grocery shopping were torture. I have frightening memories of standing weak-kneed in a shopping aisle, body frozen—too terrified to move, heart pounding, neck-breaking, having nauseated thoughts of imminent death…and everyone was watching me die. Thankfully, a loved one was always just an arm's length away to come to the rescue. They would momentarily remove me from harm's way only for the terror to return once again, again and again….

After years of anguish, the problem was eventually identified as depression and anxiety. My doctor referred me to a counselor who worked with anxiety and depression. Her treatment included behavioral therapy, group therapy and meditation. I recall the first group therapy session that I attended. Everyone jockeyed for the escape seats closest to the exit. The session nervously started as people of all walks of life began telling their stories—my story. We shared similar dark tales with excited relief, realizing that our panic was real. We no longer felt crazy and alone.

**Sharing your struggles can inspire a lifesaving journey,
coping with depression and anxiety disorder.**

CAMPFIRE

A blue flicker gently tickles the breeze
Rushing reds unlock warmth like keys.

White coals explode when aired
Flickering sparks jump as dared.

Gray smoke swirling by
Flames grow to the sky.

The fire dies leaving only blinks of light
Wishful thoughts that it once again may be bright.

CAMPFIRE *is a union of family and friends sharing a special moment in time. Campfires are truly an endearing childhood memory. Mesmerized by whimsical flames and comforted by the warmth they offered was incredibly serene. More importantly, campfires staged the sharing of dreams and blanketed all with unjudged love.*

Depression relates to the dwindling campfire, as conversations quiet and relationships fade to darkness. Sadness and despair slowly reappear as the cold night air.

Hold close the love of family and friends to rekindle the fire.

THE JUNKYARD

A field of metallic flashes
Sounds of tin clashes.

Rays of dingy color piled and bound
A chaos where value is seldom found.

Broken hope sprinkled on hills
Scurrying giants make their spills.

Coves holding secret wonders
A land of perceived blunders.

Seeing, most men's minds are barred
This world of mystery, the junkyard.

THE JUNKYARD *is perceived to be littered with unwanted things, but it can also hold objects of great value. Discarded items that were once important are often replaced by things perceived to be unavoidable. A depressed mind is much like a junkyard. Valuable positive thoughts can be discarded and replaced by negative thoughts. As depression and its adverse effects become prominent, they overpower life by eliminating an exit to happiness. As recovery begins, however, negative thoughts of depression become unimportant and are replaced by positive thoughts of value.*

Reclaim your essential positive thoughts.

THE ALMIGHTY

Silent in the heavens in some minds
Screaming in the ears of others.
Saves souls of many kinds
Loves all men like brothers.

Longing to see his way
Feeling so damn alone
Yearning for the day
When I finally arrive home.

THE ALMIGHTY *asks how a supreme being could be unkind to some men and compassionate to others. How can one worship a bias entity? For many minds, faith is an anchor. It steadies life's conflicts before they're set adrift. Others have no anchor. Negative thoughts can cause them to slowly drown without purpose.*

Depression represses personal spirituality and the compassion for self. Many relationships have ended as a result of depression. I found myself terribly alone and dealing with a demon. Faith became an important therapy for my loss of support. Religion was a positive environment that provided the compassion I desperately needed. When I began managing my depression, avenues for personal growth unlocked and optimism sparked to life.

Spirituality inspires purpose.

SANTA DIDN'T FORGET

One cold enchanting night
A tiny face stared out a window of light.
His excited eyes were locked to the sky
Waiting for Santa to pass by.

The neighbor kid, his eyes would see
Fumbling with toys under the tree,
Dejected with a saddened tear
Santa forgot me again this year.

I left cookies and even more
Daddy says he doesn't love the poor.
One cold enchanting night
A tiny face sags from sight.

The tiny face grew to be a man
Christmas memories haunted again.
No longer had sadness of a baby
Only a face of anger you could see.

Time passed and hatred grew
Deviance was all he knew.
Rebelling against society
He killed for his plea.

One cold enchanting night
A broken face peers from bars of light.

SANTA DIDN'T FORGET *is a story about happiness. As a child, my sister and I were blessed with loving parents who had the means to provide for us, especially at Christmas. Christmas was a magical time! Everything smelled fresh and clean as it was readied for guests. Treats were placed on every available surface. The house dripped with decorations inside and out. Sounds of laughter and music lofted through the halls.*

Christmas Eve dinner was typically at my grandparents' farm located in a rural area outside of town. Every Christmas Eve their house was overrun with aunts, uncles, and of course a whole slew of electrified cousins. The excitement was unbearable and I loved every second of it. However, as life happened, depression would eventually extinguish these wonderful memories. The emotions associated with my childhood happiness became lost in the darkness. The absence of childhood memories persisted for many years. It wasn't until the depression recovery treatment began that the spirit of Santa returned to my thoughts and actions.

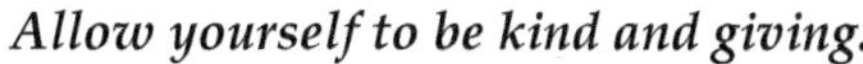

Allow yourself to be kind and giving.

BILLBOARDS

Pulsating mite of vibrant blues
Fleeting signs scream the news.

Twitching nerves of flashing whites
Drown the whispers of lavender lights.

The friendly glow of cozy reds
Calming greens weave their threads.

Screaming yellow blinds your sight
Feel the colors enhance the night.

BILLBOARDS *were once a source of great comfort. Driving the night highways was a common activity of during my depression days, or at least before anxiety stole it away. I was constantly searching for happiness and hoped to find it somewhere down the road. The billboard images that I encountered, while cruising, created a peaceful feeling of sorts. The colors and words of the billboards momentarily paused the perpetual pain of depression and calmed my anxiety.*

Practice mindfulness meditation to help keep thoughts in the present moment, like the passing billboards.

FALL OF A CHAMPION

In the modern world of towering buildings, enormous machines, and the many amazing achievements of man, the records set by nature are seldom noted but can be even more spectacular. Michigan was once home to one of the largest beech trees in the world. The tree's massive girth of 150 inches now lies limp on the compressed soil. Its height of 132 feet and crown of 116 feet litters the terrain.

The old giant braved many threats in its lifetime but none as powerful as the windstorm that battered it to the ground. The shattered bark, protruding splinters, and mutilated wood demonstrate the destruction. It now takes its last breath as massive limbs stretch skyward. A final glimpse at the height it once possessed.

Take notice of the magnificence and humble existence of a champion tree. Its broad branches are like cradling arms. They are supported by an unshakable torso. Its deep anchors clutch the earth. This amazing creation should be worshiped by man. It's truly an unselfish being, for even in death it will nourish the earth and provide a world for the next generation.

FALL OF A CHAMPION *tells the story about a large beech tree that was destroyed in a storm. I developed a great respect for this tree during the writing of a college paper. The Champion beech tree was the largest living example of its species in the region. During its life, the tree contributed numerous environmental gifts, including harboring local wildlife, controlling water runoff, conserving energy, and reducing our carbon footprint.*

The loss of this giving entity can be compared to depression. Depression destroys one's ability to fully experience life.

Even beyond tragedy, there is still great value in existence and the profound hope for a fulfilling future.

DAZED AND CONFUSED

Darkness could kill a man who is without and I could die of loneliness. Surrounded by humanity but rejected by love.

Conflicts momentarily weaken as I feel the beauty growing around me. The cool massaging breeze glides over my skin and pure misty scented air lightens the soul. I touch the moment and explore every minute object with overwhelming awe. I become a star, a cheerful wink in the heavens. I become a stalk of wheat, my structure swayed by the wind, I become an animal stepping along the edge of the moonlight, or I can become darkness killing a lonely man.

DAZED AND CONFUSED *examines a momentary taste of wonder and the yearning for socialization while traversing the murk of depression. Depression suppresses emotions needed to maintain healthy relationships.*

After my first marriage ended, I relocated to a nearby city, leaving my youngest son to finish school in his hometown. One night, I heard a knock at my apartment door. When I opened the door, there stood my smiling son and his date. They were all dressed up. Surprised, I asked, him what was going on. He said, "Just stopped by." As is turns out, my son had driven an hour to see me before attending a school prom. I felt devastated. The event was nowhere on my radar. Depression had cut off my connection with others to perpetuate self survival. The memory haunts me to this day. Such guilt. It's a painful reminder of how depression can negatively impact your life and the life of others.

As depression subsides, love and compassion will return.

SADNESS IS

Sadness is a child who will never be born
A lonely old man with a heart of scorn.

Seeing a blind man plead, hearing the jeers.
Watching his blank eyes filling with tears.

Sadness is searching for friends when friendship has died
Remembering when you lost them and how long you cried.

Sadness is passing through a fire of memories
Seeing your happiness carved in the burnt trees.

Sadness is feeling
There is no healing.

SADNESS IS *is a comparison between real-life sadness and obsessive depressive thoughts. Both are troubling, yet depression is just a perceived reality. It's a persistent negative thought pattern that can destroy all that's meaningful in life. Over time you become numbed by the struggle to survive and can offer little support to those of importance.*

Family and friends are selfishly abandoned. You have nothing left to give. Compassion and love cease to exist. The repression intensifies as shameful feelings of guilt pile up. I found myself hopelessly mired in sadness. Not until recently was it possible to acknowledge the shame and rekindle lost relationships.

Look beyond your negative thoughts to begin healing.

RIVER'S FRIEND

Sitting here on the river's lap is true peace. While its icy
waters chill my feet and they also warm my heart. I
welcome the companionship. The river's awesome power
pushes through its hardened banks. The flowing mass
torments lifeless logs, steering them helplessly in the
turbulent current. My body tumbles like a leaf battered 'mid
a foamy world. Its eruptive waters eject a thrashing spray
of enormous energy. The fine misty particles rinse my soul
as pockets of calm reflect heaven.

RIVER'S FRIEND *is a place where peace can be found.*

One of my favorite escapes from depression was to visit to an old friend, the nearby river. I spent hours acknowledging its humble existence by watching the uninhibited power flow through the weeds and propel the passing debris.

Unlike the river, depressive obsessive compulsions can restrict the normal flow of life. They reroute a confused mind into valuing unhealthy behavior. Compulsions can manifest in many ways like excessive shopping, hording, and eating. One of my compulsions was excessive cleaning. It was imperative that the house, cars, and yard were always perfectly maintained. The lawn needed to be mowed, house cleaned, and vehicles washed on a weekly basis—sometimes twice a week. Every task had to be meticulously completed before I would consider having fun. Needless to say, the tasks never got done. The compulsions created a false perception of personal value. They made me feel productive and worthwhile.

Experiences like the river overcame the devastating effects caused by compulsive actions. The beauty, sounds, and smells of nature transformed chronic actions into precious gifts of tranquility.

Welcome the calm, present moments that surround you.

A PLEA FOR LOVE

You live in my mind
Guiding my ways.
Try to be kind
Please share your days.

My heart can be broken
My feelings can be rubbed.
Need from you a token
I need to be loved.

When you were mine.
Holding close to me.
Never part in time
As one we will be.

My thoughts became sad
Not that I stopped loving you.
Feeling you're not to be had
There's nothing left to do.

Struggling to understand
Trying desperately to see.
But remember holding your hand
The kind things you said to me.

A PLEA FOR LOVE *is the yearning for the relationships alienated by a depressive state. The compassion for others is consumed by a struggle to survive the pain. People of importance become neglected and forced out of your life.*

Social anxiety controlled my life for many years. Avoiding people became a safe escape. My anxiety was particularly destructive when trying to interact with customers at work.

Talking to people created a fight-or-flight reaction. Before I could engage in conversation, the bathroom door slammed shut. There I was, like so many times before, hiding in fear, running away from me.

Interactions will improve as depression fades and frees up the emotions that support them.

WINTER'S NIGHT

Frozen white powders the earth's floor.

Cold, silent echoes of grey slumbering houses.

Scratched faded colors awakened by the moon.

The dogs bark, jerk through the frigid air.

A lonely airplane, whispering its language of blabbering lights,
animates the night sky.

It's chilling perception of the darkness, solitude, and loneliness.

Yet it offers the hopeful vision of existing.

WINTER'S NIGHT *describes a dreamlike connection with the soul. It can be a friend when you need one the most.*

Nighttime can become unbearable as the whir of the furnace and the murmurs of television fade into sadness.

Step outside and permit the healing present moments, open the black curtain of depression, and allow enlightened thoughts to illuminate the midnight gloom.

A winter's night experience will diminish bleak depressive thoughts by focusing on the positive reality.

ESCAPING

My brain ran away to a secluded shelf.
I begged him not to go.
"You can't escape the sadness," I said.
He wouldn't listen to my plea.
I told him that he needs to be with his own kind.
"You'll be lonely. Come home."
I couldn't convince him to return.
Now he sits in that desolate place.
Dust covers his reality.
Struggling in the darkness.

ESCAPING *painful thoughts is a survival mechanism associated with depression. Normal thinking and actions become overtaken by perceived negative thoughts. These negative thoughts create anxiety and eventually force a withdraw from life.*

Many meaningful events of my past were thwarted by self-created depressive anxiety. I recall an especially painful memory of a family outing. The event was an hour drive from home. The trip started out great. The car was filled with lighthearted family fun and chitchat. But, as we got closer to the venue, the what-ifs also started talking. What if I have a panic attack on the way there? What if I can't go in? What if I can stay in? I could feel the tightness in my chest. My neck stiffened to the point of breaking. I could barely catch my breath. My vision became impaired as it narrowed and blurred. No longer able to drive, I pulled into a parking lot.

Leaving my family, I stumbled out of the car and walked, and walked, and walked. I walked until death finally released its hold on me. Needless to say, we never made it to the event that night. My fears fulfilled the prophecy. All the joy was destroyed by my anxious state of mind.

Over the years the anxiety symptoms became less prominent. I began to see them as counterfeit.

Learning to accept anxiety as a negative illusion will enlighten your true reality.

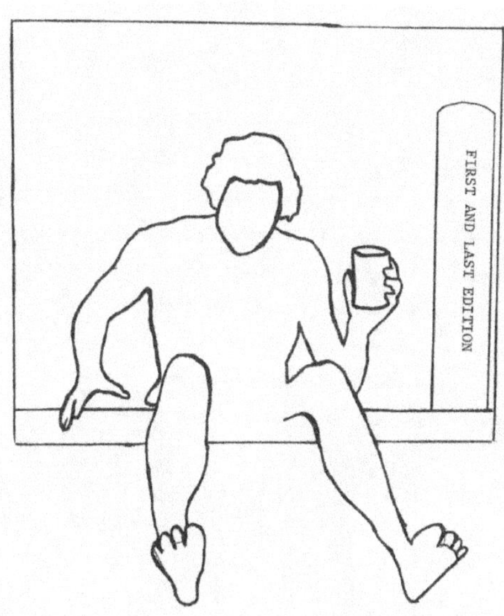

THE LETTER

Her soft eyes stepped across the trembling paper. She nervously gripped the margins. Her long brown hair fell forward as she lowered her head to see. Her eyes tried to scan words blurred by tears. Struggling to understand, she sifted through the pain again. Struggling to regain composure, she cocked her head back, closed her eyes, sighed, and sadness flowed.

THE LETTER *is a story of rejection. Feeling unwanted is a manifesting byproduct of depression. It's the fabricated fear of being negatively judged, abandoned, sick, guilty, and alone. Rejection can't be seen, smelled, heard, or touched. It's just a feeling. A powerful unforgiving feeling.*

I had a great deal of difficulty socializing as a child and well into adult life. Always felt alone in a crowd of happy souls. I was being judged. I was being rejected. I wasn't good.

When rejection can be recognized as just a negative perception, positive thinking will rewrite the letter and convey a story of unconditional love.

WATERS

The crystal aqua slowly recedes
Shallow water edged with reeds.

Wine-colored rivers polish its rocks
Forever moving cargo past the docks.

White mist dangles above crashing falls
Powerful waves pound concrete walls.

The oceans, lakes, rivers, and streams
Will live well past our final dreams.

WATERS *is a poem about life beyond pain, a future immune to the adverse feelings of depression. A beautiful healing world exists despite your negative thoughts.*

I would seek these environments to survive when my world was collapsing. They provided a needed shelter to weather the enormous pain of depression. One night while grasping the railing of a bridge, I said goodbye to my father. It was final, he was gone from my life. The feeling of being alone was unbearable. Yet, at that moment, I could hear his loving whispers from the dark water flowing under my feet.

**Nature can provide the optimism
to achieve a healthy consciousness.**

FORGIVENESS

A beautiful young leaf clings atop a towering tree. A tree whose scars represent generations of history. She exists in an ever-changing world. Her body has been wilted by the sun, drenched by rain, and strangled by wind. Faithfully she hangs on to the only thing that makes life worth living. She is content with love and being loved by the protection and nourishment she receives.

It took a storm to sever the relationship. Its winds whipped her being hopelessly about. The rain pelted her body, piercing her delicate skin like bullets spattering glass. I heard her cry, "Why are you doing this to me?!" She struggled and strained to hold on but the force was overpowering. The bond of love snapped. She fell rejected into a motionless pool of limbo. Confused, frightened, and alone. Self-pity began to weaken her structure. One day the pool took on life. The stagnant water began to move, erratically flowing outward. Its destination unknown.

The choice was hers. She could stay and resolve her problems or run away with the stream. Her mind was undecided until self-pity pushed her into its moving path. She needed to escape, to run from the pain.

She now passes by me. Her life driven by the undercurrent. Her soul relentlessly tossed by the turbulent water, her embedded dark thoughts. She presses on, always hoping, always searching for a place to forget.

I see a leaf resting on a shore far from home. Blackened waves lap over the cold damp sand. Resting gulls screech their lonely cry. The tormenting feelings relentlessly wash over her as she is helplessly trapped in the past. Yet, she fights on, praying that the new dawn will offer hope and forgiveness.

FORGIVENESS *is an important component of depression recovery. It requires transforming destructive thoughts into a conscious awakening.*

My therapist once told me, "You'll never die from a panic attack. Just allow it." This approach can be used when experiencing depressive symptoms as well. There are some days you just can't get off the couch. It's okay to feel sad and blah. Don't beat yourself up. Give yourself permission to have those feelings. I assure you, tomorrow will be better.

**By gratefully allowing your reality,
you can begin to forgive yourself.**

SUNSET

The sun sets behind the mountain and the valley becomes infested with darkness. Shadows of once lit objects are momentarily swallowed by the black.

Soon the invisible kingdom will once more be illuminated by a lunar lightbulb. Its dim glow is occasionally draped by curtains of high mist.

Daytime animals begin to dream but other creatures sound out a chorus of melodies. As the night air chills, sounds dwindle to quiet, and objects are coated with liquid dust.

Darkness has slowed life until the sun opens its eyes to awaken it.

SUNSET *reveals that even when stumbling through the darkness of depression, there is hope to light the way. The union with existence is a distraction from the pain. Mindfulness is an essential ingredient to modify negative thoughts and experience all that life has to offer.*

It can be critical finding distractions from dread when existing with depression. One night, life became hopeless. There was nowhere to turn but out the door. I traveled down the silent streets, trying to calm the horrible pain. Pausing at a crosswalk, my eyes suddenly fixed on the silhouette of a tree captured by the moonlight. Staring at the form, something appeared odd. Its branches were quivering. They appeared to be alive. I began to realize that the branches were covered with birds. Hundreds of them. Their feathers twitched as they settled in for the night. Just like that, my desperation vanished. I was experiencing life. Sharing this meeting with the birds filled me with hope and dispelled the darkness in the moonlight.

**Embracing the calm moments will inspire your life and
subdue the darkness of depression.**

JUDGMENT OF SOCIETY

I see a man
Worn in face
Holding a pan
Blank eyes pace.

I see a tear
Flowing down his cheek
Showing fear
Too terrified to speak.

One hand holds a cane
The other a pan
Society is the chain
That enslaves man.

Why do you cry
I ask myself
You're a man
Holding a pan of wealth.

JUDGMENT OF SOCIETY *speaks to the judgment and treatment of mental illness. Most people with mental illness can hide it pretty well. They avoid embarrassing judgment by quietly pretending that everything is okay or by blaming others for their actions. Some people with mental illness can live their entire life not knowing they have depression. Sadness becomes a way of life for them. Others require a great deal of nurturing, just to make it through the day. They are often rejected by health agencies and do not receive the help they need such as medications and therapy. State budget cuts have forced mental institutions to discharge patients to the streets, where they were forced to fend for themselves. With little support available, many of these individuals are unemployable and become destitute. The toxic cycle continues. Mental healthcare reform is necessary to provide the needed treatment for the mentally ill.*

Educate society about mental health and humanity will benefit.

LOOK UNDER THE BUSHES

It was the first spring-like day in southern Illinois. Fresh warm breezes circulated through opened doors and windows. People crawled out of their hibernation to enjoy the newborn season. The buzzing of lawnmowers, the teasing play of children, and the casual chants of strollers getting reacquainted could be heard echoing through the neighborhoods. Drivers rolled-down car windows to feel the excitement. Life sprouted throughout the Springfield area.

In one such town, Kellerville, sat a mother and daughter also enjoying the spring-like weather. The mother's name was Lisa. She was a very attractive young woman. She had an air of sweetness to her, calm and kind. She was young and extremely loving to her family. Lisa's daughter Amy sat on her lap. Amy's long brown hair swirled in the breeze as her big brown eyes fluttered about, taking in the spring action. Lisa sat on her mom's lap on the front porch of their Kellerville home. They were thumbing through old photographs found in a junk drawer. Lisa said, "This is your Uncle Tom when he was your age. Remember? He was the one who gave you that pretty doll for your birthday." Amy giggled. "He looks kooky with those big ears." Her mother replied, "That's not nice, but I guess he does look kind of funny." They both laughed. "Who's that, Mommy?" Lisa asked. Her mom looked where Lisa's tiny finger pointed. She sifted through the cracks and torn edges and recognized the photograph. It was picture of an old man with silver hair and a gentle smile. Lisa's face changed with emotion. Tears tricked started trickling down her cheeks. "Who is it, Mommy?" Amy asked, but Lisa didn't hear her daughter. She was overcome by her powerful memories. "Mommy! Mommy!" Amy insisted. Suddenly her mother snapped out of the trance, wiped the tears from her eyes, and said, "Oh, sorry, honey. I was just thinking. I met this nice old man when I was a little girl. He was a very special friend. He was like a grandfather to me. Well, when my daddy died my mommy and I moved to this town...." Lisa's memories became stronger. Her words were silenced but her thoughts were chronologically playing out her past....

...One warm spring day in Kellerville, Illinois, a little lonely girl named Lisa sat on her porch swing. Lisa and her mother just moved to town. Her mother just got a new job there and was busy adjusting to it. Lisa didn't know anyone. Being a shy, timid child, it was hard for her to make friends. She spent a lot of time by herself. When Amy got home from school she would scurry to the nearby park and find her favorite swing, the one with the green seat. Lisa would swing for hours and hours. Her little legs kicked as her hair streamed back and forth. Amy's rendezvous in the park became a regular routine after school. She looked forward to the freedom and companionship of her swing.

One afternoon, after Lisa got home from school, she once again headed to the park. Her tiny bare feet gingerly stepped across the rough pavement until her toes reached the soft grass of the park. Lisa scanned the playground while heading to the swings. She noticed something different, someone new. She saw a kind-looking silver-haired old man sitting near the playground. Lisa, being a shy child, wouldn't normally go near a stranger, but something drew her to him. She began feeling sad for him the closer she got. His head was drooping and appeared to be blankly staring at the ground. She started to think that the old man might be sick, lost, or maybe just lonely like her. He might need help. Lisa slowly inched her way and stood near him but the man didn't notice her. Lisa couldn't stop herself. She had to say something to the old man. So, in a tiny voice, she whispered, "Hi." Suddenly the old man's head bobbed up. He looked startled for a moment but quickly a huge grin came over his face and with a gentle voice he said, "Well, hello."

That simple interaction was all it took to begin the wonderful relationship of two lost souls. Soon the old man and Lisa were laughing and playing like best friends. The old man nicknamed Lisa "Peeper" because of her big blue eyes. Lisa called the old man Grandpa because she pictured her grandpa to be just like him. After school Lisa would anxiously run to the park and when she spotted him she would yell, "Grandpa. Grandpa!" and run into his gentle open arms. Lisa idealized him so much. She could never get enough of his stories and funny sayings. For instance, one afternoon as they both sat in the park watching the colorful clouds drift over the town of Kellerville, the old man asked, "Isn't that pretty, Peepers?" Lisa enthusiastically answered, "Yes, Grandpa." The old man looked at the clouds and said, "They remind me of when I was a little boy. Things look the same now as they did when I was a boy. Of course, those houses across the street weren't there, or this park. It was all trees and cornfields." Lisa listened attentively to his story. "I remember my grandfather waking me up early in the morning to go mushroom picking with him. He would drag me out of bed, throw on some warm clothes, and before I knew it we were headed to the kitchen. There waiting was a steaming cup of hot chocolate on the table. It tasted so good! Barely finished, he then took me by the hand, we shot out the kitchen door and headed for the barn. He swung open the squeaky barn door. I could feel the air that was warmed by a sunlit window in the tool room. He picked up an old tin bucket and threw me on his shoulders. Off to the woods we marched. Those mornings were so special. I remember birds chirping, animals scampering, and the sound of dried leaves crunching underfoot. I still remember the smell of the woods, fresh and earthy. When we finally got to his favorite place, he would put me down, and would say, 'Look underneath those bushes over there for the mushrooms.'" The old man continued. "I never really knew what I was looking for but there I was, sprawled underneath a bush, pushing leaves away, looking mushrooms." Lisa giggled, tilted her head, and asked in a puzzled voice, "Do muscooms sleep under bushes?" A grin came over the old man's face and suddenly laughter bellowed from his mouth. Trying to regain his composure, he replied, "I don't think so because every time I looked, they were never there." The silly conversation went on for a few minutes and the old man finally said, "Well, Peeper, I think it's time for you to go home." "Okay, Grampa. See you tomorrow." She started home and the old man yelled out, "Sleep tight and don't let the muscooms bite." He chucked and went on his way.

Lisa had developed a great respect for the old man. She didn't have a father and her mother was too busy trying to support them to spend much time with her. So, the old man fulfilled this void with his friendship and direction. He shared life lessons with Lisa and she clung to his every word.

The next afternoon Lisa met the old man at their usual spot after school. Holding a paper bag, he excitedly said, "Peeper, I have something for you." Lisa's eyes opened widely and she screeched, "What is it, Grandpa?" He put the bag down, opened it, and pulled out an object. Lisa stared at the object, then asked, "What is it?" The old man grinned and said, "It's a mushroom!" "A muscoom?!" Lisa excitedly replied. "Yep, I wanted to share a little of my childhood with you. Would you like to plant it here in the park?" Lisa shouted back, "Sure. Where are we going to plant it,

Grandpa?" The old man raised his head to scope out the area and then pointed.

"How about under that bush?" Lisa agreed. "It will be a safe place for it to sleep tonight." The old man laughed and said, "Okay. Let's go plant our mushroom, Peeper." He took her by the hand and strolled over to the bush. Gasping and straining, he knelt down. Looking at the soil, he pointed and said, "Scoop a little hole in the dirt." She crawled underneath the bush and with her tiny fingers dug a small hole. "That's good," the old man praised. "Put the mushroom in the hole and cover its roots with dirt." Lisa carefully did what he said. She sat up, smiled, and asked, "Is that good?" "You did just fine," the old man replied. Lisa gazed at the mushroom for a moment, then asked, "Will it be okay tonight, Grandpa? Will it live?" He convincingly replied, "It will live as sure as I will see you tomorrow." She looked relieved. It was getting late, so the old man and Lisa said their goodbyes.

The following day when Lisa got home from school, she briefly greeted her mother and then ran out the door, headed to the park. She couldn't wait to see her friend, the old man. Arriving at the park, her big blue eyes looked for the silver-haired old man. First making a beeline for the place where they always met, the swings, but he wasn't there. She started running through the park, looking behind every tree, but couldn't find him. Becoming more and more uneasy, she began to call out, "Grandpa! Grandpa! Where are you, Grandpa?" Her eyes frantically kept searching. But, then she remembered the mushroom. Running to the bush, she fell to her knees and crawled underneath. Hoping to see the mushroom but all she could see was a shriveled object. The mushroom was gone. Lisa's face flushed with disbelief. Suddenly she recalled what the old man said the day before: "It will live as sure as I will see you tomorrow." Terrified, Lisa crawled to her feet. With tears flowing down her cheeks, she ran home. Sobbing, Lisa worked open the door and cried out, "Mommy! Mommy! Mommy! Mommy!" Amy impatiently tried to get her mother's attention. Moments passed and still no answer. Lisa, with her tear-glazed eyes, was still recalling the painful memory of the loss of her friend, the old man. Amy once again shouted, "Mommy! There's someone here to see you. He said his name is Grandpa and an old friend of yours."

LOOK UNDER THE BUSHES *is my childhood story. I would tag along with my grandfather on those frosty mornings to go mushrooming. It was a time of wonder, imagination, and of happiness. It was also a time of despair.*

At an early age, seclusion and sadness began to plague me. Playing alone and avoiding family events became the norm. My self-conscious walls blocked most relationships other than family and friends. The fear of negative judgment corrupted my happiness from early childhood until very recently. Retirement provided the necessary time to work on depression recovery. With a new determination and learned cognitive behavioral skills, the darkness began to recede. I'm able to begin dealing with the guilt and anger of the past, and allow myself to be happy, living gratefully in the present. Life is now available to enjoy.

Recall your happy memories.

PIERCING THE DARKNESS

Eyes open
Fog clears.
Images focus
Hope appears.

Forgiveness enabled
Acceptance dwells.
Compassion grows
Love swells.

Enrichment builds
Optimism soars.
Enthusiasm returns
Creativity roars.

Contentment breathes
Happiness wins.
Gratitude serves.
Life begins! Life begins! Life begins!

PIERCING THE DARKNESS *reflects on my youthful, depressive poetry, providing valuable insights into a challenging journey that spanned decades. The wisdom gained strengthened my desire to pursue an important purpose—to be alive. Passions returned with mind-dancing ideas. Words shouted the newfound freedom. Childhood memories played once again. Relationships rebuilt a precious history. Awakened emotions excited the senses, leaving me breathless amid every unending moment. My aging body and mind are graced with new opportunities.*

**Start now. Do the work and be amazed at your potential.
You'll love what comes next!**

REVIEW

"What a gift of a book! I was moved to read these reflections across decades of struggle and insight. Thank you for sharing this vulnerable work- it makes me feel less alone and makes me want to keep moving outside of myself and towards the world, while we still have time! I'm really lucky to share some of your sensitivity, grace, and fortitude. Looking for all that lies ahead."

Jason Sudak
Instructor of Arts of the Moving Image
Duke University
& my son

REFLECTING
by Cindy

REFLECTING
ON PERSONAL SADNESS
WHILE CREATING SELF BARRIERS
CAUSING SOCIAL CHALLENGES

OPENING
UP TO OTHERS
WITH INSPIRATIONAL HELP BY SHARING
AND HEALING OLD WOUNDS

MOLDING
A STRONGER MAN
AS WELL AS A CARING FATHER
AND LOVING HUSBAND

CELEBRATING
ALL THAT YOU WERE
LEADING THE WAY TO ALL THAT YOU ARE
A VERY SPECIAL, 65 YEAR OLD, REALISTIC MAN

LOVE
CINDY

Original 1977 Back Cover